Ulf Wakenius:
MODERN**SAXOPHONE**LICKS
FORJAZZ**GUITAR**

Master the Soloing Language of Post-Bop & Modern Saxophone Legends on Jazz Guitar

ULF**WAKENIUS**

With Tim Pettingale

FUNDAMENTAL**CHANGES**

Ulf Wakenius: Modern Saxophone Licks for Jazz Guitar

Master the Soloing Language of Post-Bop & Modern Saxophone Legends on Jazz Guitar

ISBN: 978-1-78933-381-7

Published by **www.fundamental-changes.com**

www.fundamental-changes.com

Over 12,000 fans on Facebook: **FundamentalChangesInGuitar**

Instagram: **FundamentalChanges**

For over 350 Free Guitar Lessons with Videos Check Out

www.fundamental-changes.com

Cover Image Copyright: Author photo, used by permission

Contents

About the Author

Swedish guitarist Ulf Wakenius was born in Halmstad and raised in Gothenburg. Throughout his career he has played a wide range of music, but is best known for his straight ahead and post-bop jazz. Ulf studied at the Gothenburg Conservatoire and was soon working as a session musician in his teens. He was a member of the Swedish bands Sundance and Mwendo Dawa and in the early 1980s formed the duo Guitars Unlimited with Peter Almqvist, releasing two albums. During this period, he also began working with renowned bass player Niels-Henning Ørsted Pedersen, a collaboration that continued until Ørsted Pedersen's death in 2005.

Ulf was a member of the group Grafitti with Dennis Chambers (drums), Gary Grainger (bass) and Haakon Graf (keys), which released the 1992 album *Good Groove*. The same year Ulf released the album *Venture* as leader, with a line-up that included Chris Minh Doky, Niels Lan Doky, Randy Brecker, Lars Danielsson, Bob Berg, saxophonist Bill Evans, and Jack DeJohnette. Ulf also led the Stellar Quintet which included Michael Brecker and Ray Brown.

Ulf played on two recordings for Ray Brown, *Seven Steps to Heaven* (1995) and *Summertime* (1997). In 1997 he joined Oscar Peterson's quartet, which included Ørsted Pedersen on bass and Martin Drew on drums, and toured the world with Oscar for the next decade.

He has worked with many other notable jazz musicians, including Herbie Hancock, Joe Henderson, Art Farmer and Clark Terry to name just a few. He continues to tour and record with a variety of collaborators and in 2017 he joined his son, guitarist Eric Wakenius, for the duo album *Father & Son*.

What others have said about Ulf...

"He plays the guitar like he was born with it already in his hands." – **John McLaughlin**

"Just great!" – **Pat Metheny**

"So you are the bad boy everybody's talking about?!" – **Larry Carlton**

"Spectacular! Unbelievable!" – **Allan Holdsworth**

"I heard you with Ray Brown, you sounded great!" – **John Scofield**

"Humongous chops!" – **Pat Martino**

Introduction

Learning to play modern jazz is like learning any language. If you want to learn it in a useful manner you need a phrasebook not a dictionary. The ideal way to begin learning is to have a specific context and to learn complete phrases that relate to it.

This approach will get you so far – a basic working grasp of the language – but if you want to really master the language, you need to get alongside some native speakers and hear how they use it in a variety of situations. Invariably, they will quickly be able to show you what you need to know (and what not to waste your time learning) and point out the finer nuances of language that a phrasebook won't give you.

This book is study of the jazz language of some of the great modern post-bop saxophonists. It follows on from my previous book, *Bebop Saxophone Licks for Jazz Guitar*. In that volume, we studied essential licks in the style of Charlie Parker, Stan Getz, Sonny Rollins, Ben Webster and Cannonball Adderley. In this volume we are going to tackle the melodic language of five players who were fundamental in pushing forward the evolving sound of modern jazz:

John Coltrane, Joe Henderson, Wayne Shorter, Michael Brecker and Joshua Redman.

But this is not just a book of licks. We're going to look at *why* these musicians played the ideas they did on some of their most iconic recordings. My aim is to equip you with lots of great jazz lines that work over the changes to some famous standards, but I also want to give you an insight into the melodic/harmonic devices used by the greats to create those lines.

We can learn from any great jazz instrumentalist, and these master saxophonists have lots to teach us about phrasing, time, how to create and develop motif-based solos, and how to apply simple techniques to get that modern "outside-inside" sound that weaves around the harmony.

I really enjoyed putting this book together and I hope you enjoy the journey too!

Ulf.

Get the Audio

The audio files for this book are available to download for free from **www.fundamental-changes.com.** The link is in the top right-hand corner. Click on the "Guitar" link then simply select this book title from the drop-down menu and follow the instructions to get the audio.

We recommend that you download the files directly to your computer, not to your tablet, and extract them there before adding them to your media library. You can then put them onto your tablet, iPod or burn them to CD. On the download page there are instructions and we also provide technical support via the contact form.

For over 350 free guitar lessons with videos check out:

www.fundamental-changes.com

Join our free Facebook Community of Cool Musicians

www.facebook.com/groups/fundamentalguitar

Tag us for a share on Instagram: **FundamentalChanges**

Chapter One – John Coltrane

Quick bio

John William Coltrane – *Trane* to his friends – was born on September 23, 1926, in Hamlet, North Carolina. His father, a part-time musician, was one of his earliest influences. In June 1943 the Coltrane family moved to Philadelphia and that September his mother bought John an alto saxophone. By mid-1945 he was playing his first professional gigs in a cocktail lounge trio with piano and guitar.

He switched to tenor saxophone in 1947 and during the late 40s and early 50s was playing in nightclubs and recording with a variety of musicians, but notably Dizzy Gillespie. Coltrane achieved much wider recognition when he joined the Miles Davis quintet in 1955.

The years 1955 to 1957 were his "Miles and Monk" period. He was part of Miles' "first great quintet" with bandmates Red Garland (piano), Paul Chambers (bass) and Philly Joe Jones (drums). While this time was musically fruitful, it was personally difficult for Trane, and the quintet disbanded due to his heroin addiction.

In the latter part of 1957, Coltrane was working with Thelonious Monk and made some seminal recordings included the highly rated *Thelonious Monk Quartet with John Coltrane at Carnegie Hall*. The same year, Coltrane recorded one of his most iconic recordings as a leader for Blue Note records: *Blue Train*, released in 1958. Coltrane also re-joined Miles in 1958 and stayed with him until 1960, during which time he worked on the recordings of *Milestones* and *Kind of Blue*.

Coltrane was a hard-working musician who paid his dues as a sideman and kept up a prodigious practice regime. He went on to release twenty-five albums as a leader, many of which are essential listening for every jazz musician, and are important landmarks in the history and development of modern jazz, especially *Blue Train, Giant Steps, My Favorite Things* and the Grammy nominated *A Love Supreme*.

In 2007 Trane was posthumously awarded a Pulitzer Prize as a Special Citation for a lifetime of innovative and influential work. He is simply one of the most towering iconic figures of 20th Century jazz.

Characteristics of Coltrane's style

One of the things always mentioned about Coltrane is the breathtaking practice regime he maintained, which has been described as "obsessive" and even "maniacal". He studied Nicolas Slonimsky's *Thesaurus of Scales and Melodic Patterns,* constantly listened to jazz and transcribed countless solos. He would practice late into the night, just rehearsing fingering patterns when blowing into his sax would have upset his sleeping neighbours.

Broadly speaking, Coltrane's musical development can be understood in three distinct phases: his "sheets of sound", modal, and free jazz periods. "Sheets of sound" was a term coined by music critic Ira Gitler for the liner notes of the *Soultrane* album to describe Coltrane's improvisational technique at the time, which was based around layering extended, altered and substitute arpeggios over complex chord changes.

Our snapshot of Coltrane's style is taken from his modal period where he was experimenting with the sound of modal scales and using shifting tonal centres to open things up harmonically and give him more melodic options. The sparse chord changes of modal tunes provided a stark contrast to the rich harmonies of bebop but served to give improvisers the space and license to explore ideas that wouldn't otherwise have been possible. During this period Coltrane still worked with layered arpeggios as part of his experimentation.

One aspect of Coltrane's playing that has been discussed and copied a great deal is his use of four-note patterns, now known simply as "Coltrane patterns". The essence of this idea is to use four notes to spell out the sound of a chord. Since a great deal of jazz soloing features consistent 1/8th note passages, it's a very useful approach to be able to construct melodic lines from cells of four notes then string them together. You can clearly hear Coltrane using this approach when soloing over his classic *Giant Steps*, where the chord changes move very quickly, and the key changes are not necessarily intuitive.

We could spend an entire book discussing Coltrane changes, but here is the concept in very simplified form. Coltrane had a four-note melodic formula that he played on each chord type. Here are the major and minor chord interval structures:

The Major four-note pattern is: 1, 2, 3, 5

The Minor four-note pattern is: 1, b3, 4, 5

In the key of C Major, the Coltrane pattern for a C major chord would therefore be:

C D E G

Of course, we don't have to play those four notes in the same order every time. We can re-sequence the pattern to become 5 1 2 3, or 2 1 5 3 etc, to create different phrases.

So far so good, now let's take this idea a step further…

In this chapter, the licks are played over the changes to Coltrane's tune *Impressions*. This is a modal tune comprising just two chords and spends the majority of its time vamping on a Dm7 chord.

The mood of the piece has a Dorian vibe, so Dm7 is seen as chord ii in the parent key of C Major. What implications does this have for applying Coltrane patterns?

We can use the minor four-note pattern described above, which will be made up of:

D (1), F (b3), G (4), A (5)

Then we can change the order of that sequence, as we've discussed.

However, in the key of C Major there are three major triads, three minor triads and one diminished triad:

- C major, F major, G major

- D minor, E minor, A minor

- B diminished

Coltrane would draw from *all* of these triads, then use combinations of them to solo. Any of these forms can be played over Dm7 and each will produce its own particular intervallic sound.

Superimposing a G major triad over Dm7, for instance, adds the sounds of the 11th (G) and 13th (B) intervals.

Superimposing an E minor triad adds the 9th (E), as well as the 11th (G) and 13th (B).

Using the diatonic triads of the parent scale, Coltrane would create a four-note pattern for each one, using his pattern formulas. Here's an example of his thinking:

Remember that the parent scale is C Major scale, which has the notes: C D E F G A B

Let's take the G major triad. Treating the G note as 1, Coltrane would apply the major 1 2 3 5 pattern to produce a G A B D cell. This gives us the notes of the G major triad (G B D) plus an A note.

He would construct a similar four-note pattern for every triad, using his different formulas.

Pause for a moment and consider the fact that each of the six triads in the scale can be turned into a four-note cell, and that each cell can then be played in many different sequences over a single chord, and you will see that Coltrane's logic leads to a mind-boggling array of melodic options. Now you can understand why he was up all night practicing!

Coltrane would also combine these cellular forms with scale runs, so in the examples that follow you'll see four-note patterns blended with occasional scalic lines and also broken up rhythmically.

The scale used here is D Dorian (D E F G A B C) – like playing a C Major scale beginning and ending on D.

Iconic Recording: Impressions

Impressions, composed by Coltrane in 1961, is one of his most well-known tunes and a jam session favourite. Coming from the album of the same name, it was recorded live at the Village Vanguard club in New York, with McCoy Tyner on piano, Jimmy Garrison on bass and Elvin Jones on drums. This version of the tune is 15 minutes long and features an epic, extended solo.

The form of *Impressions* is as follows:

Dm7 x 16 bars

Ebm7 x 8 bars

Dm7 x 8 bars

The challenge of playing this tune can be simply counting the bars and knowing where you are in the tune, as the eight bars of Dm7 that conclude the tune are followed by another sixteen bars of Dm7 when you loop back to the top.

All the examples here are played over Dm7 but they can, of course, be transposed up a half-step to work over Ebm7.

John Coltrane vocabulary for jazz guitar

Now let's explore some Coltrane-type vocabulary over this modal tune. Sometimes this tune has been played at breakneck tempo, but here we are working with a more chilled, moody vibe, which makes it easier to absorb and understand his ideas.

In this first example, the first four bars use the D minor Coltrane pattern but the 5th (A) is left out and it has just the root (D), b3 (F) and 4th/11th (G).

In bars 5-8, we turn to D Dorian scale-based ideas and a B note is highlighted several times to imply the underlying harmony is Dm6 (D F A B). In bar nine, the first four notes are a re-sequenced D minor Coltrane pattern (5 b3 1 4).

Example 1a

This next line is built around a repeating motif. For the melodic line in bars 1-4, all the notes come from a Bm7b5 arpeggio (B D F A). Bm7b5 is chord vii in the parent key of C Major. It's the idea of superimposing triads/arpeggios from the same key to create a different musical effect. Notice that Bm7b5 contains the root, b3 and 5th of D minor, plus the 6th. In bars 5-7 we move to a descending D Dorian scale sequence.

Example 1b

In the next example, more superimposed arpeggios give the line an unresolved feeling. In bar one, the notes come from the G major Coltrane pattern, but avoid the G root. Bar two uses a G major triad inversion and in bar three, we're back to the Bm7b5 arpeggio. From bar four to the end, we're thinking scalically again and the line ends on the 6th of D minor.

Example 1c

This next example contains a lick Coltrane would often play. In begins in bar five and spills into bar six. It's a simple idea: start on the root of the D Dorian scale and ascend in 3rds. However, the line begins on the second beat of the bar so that it crosses the bar line to include the two 1/8th notes in bar six. In bar seven, string skips add to the intervallic feel of the lick as it descends towards the D root note.

Example 1d

Bar one of the next line spells an E minor triad, bar two an F major triad, and bar three is the 6th, root and 5th of D minor. The five-note phrase in bar four spells out the sound of a Dm13 chord, omitting the root and 9th. This idea repeats in bar five, with the notes in a different order.

Bars 6 and 7 return to a more scalic idea, with bar six containing the first chromatic passing note we've encountered so far. Its role here is to add a moment of tension and resolution. As the line ends in bar eight, we have another passing note as we land on an Eb rather than the D root. An idea like this can cause surprise, as the listener will expect to hear a resolution to the "home" sound. In this tune, it could also be used to anticipate the arrival of the bridge section that modulates up to Eb minor.

In your practice sessions, start to think about how you can break up your lines by mixing scale runs with shorter, triadic or four-note cell statements. It's a simple but effective strategy to freshen up your playing.

Example 1e

The next example consists entirely of four-note cells. Each idea is drawn from the parent key of C Major to superimpose different tonalities over the Dm7 chord. In bar one it's F major then E minor. Bar two uses F major and G major. Bar three focuses on the Bm7b5 vii chord, and bar four uses E minor then a Dm6 arpeggio, sequenced into a 5 1 3 6 pattern.

Notice how this line weaves around the harmony because the D root note doesn't land on the beat until bar four.

Example 1f

Example 1g is the first line that really takes advantage of chromatic passing notes to create a truly "outside-inside" line that pushes the harmony and challenges the ears.

Let's investigate what's happening here.

In bar one, we have a question and answer type phrase. The opening four-note cell is an F major superimposition. The "answer" phrase in the second half uses a C# passing note and hints at the sound of a Dm(Maj)7 tonality (D F A C#).

Bars 2-3 use superimposed arpeggios to construct the four-note phrases. In order, they are Am11, G major, F major and G major again.

The first half of bar four is a B diminished triad with one note repeated to create the four-note pattern. Then comes the start of a tense, outside phrase than spans into bar five.

The second half of bar four, which begins this phrase uses a simple "side-stepping" idea. Two D Dorian scale notes are played (A and D), which are then shifted in a half-step movement in contrary motion. The D is lowered a half-step to Db, while the A is raised a half-step to Bb.

In bar five, after the initial C scale note, the purpose of the phrase is to descend chromatically, targeting the F note that falls on beat 1 of bar six. Bars 6-7 return to D minor four-note cells, with bar seven spelling a Dm6.

Example 1g

While Coltrane frequently built small cellular ideas from arpeggios and connected them, he would, of course, also use straight scalic licks too. The phrase in bar one of the next example is a textbook bebop lick using the D Melodic Minor scale (D E F G A B C#) and includes a passing C note.

In bar two, the melodic line moves to another side-stepping idea. The first four notes come from D Dorian. These are played around 5th position and the next four notes arise from shifting up a half-step. It's a simple way of moving outside, and one which we can easily resolve back to an inside line.

Bar three creates the same effect. We could analyse the effect of these notes over the Dm7 chord, but the line is really about taking advantage of the geography of the fretboard, taking a simple pattern we know fits over the chord, then moving it outside.

All this tension is resolved in the second half of bar four as we return to a D minor shape.

Example 1h

Here's a Coltrane-inspired idea that uses only the notes of the D Dorian scale. In bars 1-2 the B on the 2nd string 12th fret is emphasised to imply a Dm6 harmony (D F A B). From bar four onwards, it's a case of sequencing D Dorian into 1/8th note groups of four that ascend and descend. At the end of bar eight the line ends on the B note again.

Example 1i

To end our look at Coltrane vocabulary, here's one more side-stepping idea. It was inspired by playing around a 5th position D minor chord shape before moving up a half-step to play an array of notes in 6th position and add tense, outside tones.

Bar five features a D Melodic Minor lick as we begin to complete the line, and bar six is a D Dorian idea that uses chromatic passing notes to add a bluesy enclosure at the beginning.

Example 1j

To continue working on Coltrane-style licks, make a Dm7 chord loop for yourself, or find one on YouTube, and experiment with the idea of playing different diatonic arpeggios over it using simple shapes.

Also spend some time drilling basic arpeggio patterns and sequences. If you know your arpeggio shapes across the neck, Coltrane's superimposition ideas will do the hard work of producing some cool sounding lines for you.

Chapter Two – Joe Henderson

Quick bio

Joe Henderson was born in Lima, Ohio, on April 24, 1937, and came from a large family with six sisters and nine brothers. His parents and older brother James (also a saxophonist) encouraged him to study music, and his early efforts included piano, saxophone and drums. He spent time engrossed in his brother's record collection and a drummer from the family's hometown urged him to check out saxophonists such as Charlie Parker, Stan Getz, Dexter Gordon and Lester Young.

Young and Parker were his biggest inspirations, although Henderson certainly created his own unique style. By 18, he was gigging in Detroit's jazz scene, and while studying music at Wayne State University he built on his saxophone chops under the expert guidance of master saxophonist Larry Teal. When he arrived at the university, he had transcribed and memorised so many of Lester Young's solos that his tutors assumed he had perfect pitch! In Detroit he built a reputation for being a fearless soloist, and drew the attention and praise of such luminaries as Sonny Stitt, Dexter Gordon and John Coltrane.

After serving in the army from 1960-62, Henderson was signed to Blue Note records and also produced several albums for Milestone Records. During his life he recorded nearly 40 albums as leader and played on many more as a sideman. He recorded with Herbie Hancock, did a short stint with Miles Davis, and was a member of Horace Silver's quintet from 1964-66 (playing on Silver's classic recording, *Song for my Father*). He also played on Lee Morgan's iconic album, *The Sidewinder*.

In the 1970s, Henderson played for a time with jazz-rock group *Blood Sweat & Tears*, and continued to make albums as a leader throughout the 1980s. During this time, he released a two-disc album with Blue Note called *The State of the Tenor, Vol. 1 & 2: Live at the Village Vanguard*, with Ron Carter on bass and Al Foster on drums.

Henderson won a Grammy for Best Instrumental Jazz Soloist for *Lush Life* from *Lush Life: The Music of Billy Strayhorn* in 1992. He also won two Grammy awards in 1993: Best Jazz Instrumental Soloist for *Miles Ahead* and Best Jazz Instrumental Group for *So Near, So Far: Musings for Miles*. A fourth Grammy came in 1997 for Best Large Jazz Ensemble Performance for Henderson's album *Big Band*.

Joe Henderson was a highly influential figure in the development of modern jazz, and two of the players we'll explore in this book – Michael Brecker and Joshua Redman – cite him as a major influence.

Characteristics of Henderson's style

Guitarist John Scofield said of Henderson in a *DownBeat* magazine interview, "Joe Henderson is the essence of jazz. He's a great blues player, a great ballads player … he's got unbelievable time. He can float, but he can also dig in. He's got his own vocabulary … he'll play a blues shout like something by Joe Turner next to some of the fastest, 'outest', most angular, most atonal music you've ever heard. Who's playing better on any instrument, more interestingly, more cutting edge yet completely with 'roots' than Joe? He's my role model."

Henderson's playing has been described as an extension of the style of Sonny Rollins. The legacy of bebop is present in his playing, but Henderson took the saxophone to new technical levels. Dave Liebman said that he played with unending variations of articulation and a looseness that defied the bar line. It's these qualities of Henderson's playing that we'll explore in this chapter.

As you work through the licks below, you'll notice that Henderson-style playing places an emphasis on developing melodic motifs with a command of rhythmic variety. Combine these two elements and you have a powerful storytelling approach.

Iconic Recording: Blues Bossa

The reference track for this chapter is *Blue Bossa*. Written by Kenny Dorham, it appears on the 1963 album *Page One*. Henderson's band for this album comprised Kenny Dorham (trumpet), McCoy Tyner (piano), Butch Warren (bass) and Pete LaRoca (drums).

Dorham's tune has become one of the all-time most popular jazz standards, so listening to what a master player like Henderson has to say over the tune's relatively simple harmony is an education. The piece was originally written around the bassline, which drives the groove of the piece and glues everything together, and original sheet music for the tune has it written alongside the melody.

Henderson commented that he was always inspired by Dorham's writing and enjoyed how he wrote for the rhythm section when composing. Henderson used this idea himself; his tune *Recorda Me*, which also appears on the *Page One* album, is also written around a bassline.

Blue Bossa is a great tune to play on guitar as each melody note fall beautifully around common guitar chord inversions and includes minor sixths and quartal chords. Here is the structure of the tune in the key of C minor:

It begins with a chord I to IV progression followed by a ii V i where the V chord is a dominant 7, usually played as a G7b9 or G7#5.

| Cm7 | % | Fm7 | % |

| Dm7b5 | G7b9 | Cm7 | % |

The tune then modulates up a minor third for a ii V I in Db Major. To turn the tune back around to C Minor, the Dbmaj7 becomes Dm7b5 (on guitar you only need to move one finger to accomplish this change).

| Ebm7 | Ab7 | Dbmaj7 | % |

| Dm7b5 | G7b9 | Cm7 | % |

Joe Henderson vocabulary for jazz guitar

Now let's explore how some of Joe Henderson's vocabulary can be applied on guitar.

This first line is an example of Henderson's strident rhythmic approach. The 1/8th note motif set up in bar one is played very straight over the bossa nova beat of *Blue Bossa*, so that it "rubs" against the timing in an attention-grabbing manner.

Here, the C Dorian scale is played throughout. In bar three, the motif repeats exactly as in bars 1-2. In bar one, the lick emphasises the C root note. Over the Fm7, the C becomes the 5th, so this simple idea works perfectly well to outline the changes.

Henderson will sometimes imply harmony using very few notes and bar five is an example of this. Still using just C Dorian, the G note is an unusual but richly harmonic choice over Dm7b5. G is the 11th and the F note that follows is the b3. Layered over the chords of the accompanist, it implies the sound of Dm11b5.

A similar thing occurs over the G7 chord in bar six. The opening four notes are carefully selected from the scale and all but the G root are extensions of the chord. They are the b13 (Eb), 11th (C) and 9th (A), in order of appearance.

Example 2a

Example 2b illustrates the type of Henderson line John Scofield described as "floating" over the time. It's a cool, laid back lick. Bars 1-5 show that it's possible to outline the harmony with just a few notes, allowing plenty of space, and the simple motif is relocated to fit over the Fm7.

Bars 6-7 move into bebop language territory. For these bars, C Melodic Minor (C D Eb F G A B) is the scale of choice. The Ab note at the end of bar six is a chromatic approach note that anticipates the G on the first beat of bar seven. A Db to D chromatic approach adds to the bebop flavour of the line.

Example 2b

The next example also begins sparsely. Bars 1-2 contain a question and answer phrase, with the answer stated in the lower register.

In bar four, a simple rhythmic idea is stated: a three-note phrase that combines a pair of 1/16th notes and an 1/8th note. Henderson is perhaps the most explorative of the players in this book. He's not afraid to introduce a simple idea, then leave space to think about what he's going to do with it. The Dm7b5 chord (bar five) is left silent, then the three-note phrase bursts into action over G7. The harmony is adventurous too. The Ab note on the 1& of bar six is the b9 of G7 and the later Db is the b5.

In bars 7-8 comes a typical Henderson-ism: a sudden, surprising rhythmic lick. Ideas like this can add drama to your phrasing and we'll hear similar ideas as we progress.

Example 2c

One thing that really stands out about Joe Henderson's playing is his ability to craft a perfect phrase. The line that spans bars 1-2 uses C Melodic Minor and in bar two the note choices make a point of highlighting the flavour of this scale. The A and B notes are what distinguishes C Melodic Minor from the C Natural Minor scale (which has an Ab and Bb). Over a Cm7 chord, the A implies a Cm13 harmony, and the B implies CmMaj7.

The melodic line is shifted upwards to be played over the Fm7 in bars 3-4 to the same effect. The E and D notes highlight that we're playing F Melodic Minor here, not F Natural Minor.

Notice the lick over the G7 chord in bar six. It's a four-note phrase that is repeated an octave lower. Before you learn the whole line, look at this bar in isolation. Play a basic three-note G7 chord in 10th position, then with your fourth finger, superimpose each of the four notes in turn. You'll probably see that the Eb is the #5 of G7, the B is a repeat of the 3rd, the A# is the #9, and the Ab is the b9.

Example 2d

The next example is played over the bridge section of the tune, which shifts up a minor third. It demonstrates how Henderson's style gets maximum return from a very simple idea. The entire lick consists of just four notes that spell a Dbmaj7 arpeggio (Db F Ab C).

It is never arpeggiated from the root, but from the 7th in two alternating sequences: C Db F Ab and C Ab F Db. The arpeggio notes have a different effect over each chord. The leading C note is the 13th over Ebm7 and the 3rd of Ab7.

It would be tempting to begin an idea like this on the first beat of the bar, but typically Henderson will displace it, so here it starts on beat three and floats across the bar line.

Example 2e

Next up is a modern sounding lick that blends together and sequences two complementary scales. The line is constructed using four-note cells from C Melodic Minor and C Natural Minor that switch between each other to form a descending pattern. This approach is continued over the Fm7 chord in bar three. The last note (the Ab of C Natural Minor) is the b3 of Fm7.

Example 2f

Next, let's have a look at a melodic line that spans the bridge section of the tune. Space is left in bar one, and the lick begins on the "1&" of bar two. In bar two, the common substitution idea of playing off the minor ii chord of the dominant 7 is used, so the lick begins with an Eb minor triad, raked upwards from the 1st string. In bar three, the downward raked triplets spell out Ab and Db major triads.

Example 2g

Example 2h showcases a Henderson-style line based around his aggressive rhythmic approach. If you listen to his solos, you'll often find similar dramatic rhythmic statements, with space left around them so that the impact of a sudden burst of rhythm is allowed to sink in. In bar one, emphasis is placed on the G (the 5th of Cm7), played as an enclosure.

The phrasing is repeated over the Fm7 chord, but this time the emphasis is on the 6th (D), to imply an Fm6 sound. For the Dm7b5 chord, a similar idea continues, with an Ab chord tone at the centre of the enclosure and the rhythm changed from 1/16th notes to 1/8th note triplets.

In bar six the phrase from bar five is continued briefly. Over a G7 chord, the emphasised Ab note is the b9. In the latter half of the bar, a G augmented triad resolves to the Cm7 chord.

This type of idea shows the value of experimenting with rhythm. As guitarists, we often default not only to tried and tested licks, but also rhythms. It's easy to miss the dynamism that rhythmic variety can add to our playing.

Example 2h

Here is another example of the way in which Joe Henderson used rhythm to command the listener's attention and create angular, modern lines.

The lick is arranged to take advantage of 4th intervals on the guitar. In bar one, the line begins on the b7 of Cm7, and begins on the 1& of the bar to make things more unpredictable. I play this line with my first finger barred across the bottom three strings at the 6th fret, then slide the barre up to the 8th. I use my fourth finger to play the G on the 10th fret.

In bars 3-4, this idea gets transferred across to strings 5, 4 and 3 for the Fm7 chord, again launching from the b7.

In bar five, a C Aeolian scale sequence is arranged as an ascending run, still taking advantage of 4th intervals.

When we get to bar six, a well-known bebop scale substitution idea is used to create tension. It's common to substitute a minor scale whose root is a half-step above a dominant 7 chord, i.e. Ab minor over G7. Bebop practitioners have long used this idea to quickly capture an altered sound. Here the Ab Melodic Minor scale is used. Superimposed over G7 it instantly creates the sound of the G Altered Scale.

Example 2i

In our final Joe Henderson-style example, we return to his love of motif-driven lines. A simple motif idea outlines the Cm7 and Fm7 chords. In bar five, a staple bebop lick outlines the Dm7b5 chord and in bar six, extensions of G7 are used to add flavour, beginning with the b5 and including the #9. The line targets a D to imply a cool Cm9 to finish.

Example 2j

In your practice sessions, try taking a simple lick and varying its rhythm. Experiment with this idea and don't hold back! Move it to different beats of the bar, break it up, and try it over different chords. Often, the discipline of thoroughly exploring one idea will spark new creativity.

Chapter Three – Wayne Shorter

Quick bio

Wayne Shorter was born on August 25, 1933, in Newark, New Jersey. He was encouraged to take up the clarinet by his father when he was 16 but switched to tenor saxophone before entering New York University in 1952. After graduation in 1956, he played with Horace Silver before being drafted into the Army. Once he had completed his service, he joined Maynard Ferguson's band where he met pianist Joe Zawinul, who would later become his Weather Report bandmate.

Before then, however, he would play with both Art Blakey's Jazz Messengers and Miles Davis' quintet. While accompanying Miles through his transition from post-bop into electric jazz-rock, Shorter also took up soprano saxophone – a sound that was able to cut through the mix of an electric band better than tenor. Many music critics have noted that Shorter sounds like a completely different player on soprano to tenor.

Weather Report was formed in 1970 and Shorter would play with the band for the next sixteen years, with the group collecting six Grammy Awards along the way. They were pioneers of jazz fusion and included elements of ethnic folk music, RnB, funk and rock in their music. During this time, Shorter pared back his style in favour of supporting the band's compositions, playing much more economically.

Post Weather Report, Shorter has continued to lead various bands and has collaborated with musicians including Herbie Hancock, Ron Carter, Marcus Miller and Carlos Santana. In 2000 he formed a permanent acoustic group as leader with Danilo Perez on piano, John Patitucci on bass and Brian Blade on drums, and to date they have released four live albums, winning the Grammy Award for Best Instrumental Jazz Album for 2006's *Beyond the Sound Barrier*.

Shorter is considered to be the greatest living jazz composer and has 10 Grammy Awards to his name, along with a lifetime achievement Grammy, five honorary doctorates, and numerous other awards and accolades for his contribution to music.

Characteristics of Shorter's style

There is no doubt that Wayne Shorter's playing has embraced a wide spectrum of modern jazz, moving through hard bop to modal jazz to becoming a pioneer of jazz fusion. Shorter is also a great composer and this skill carries through into his soloing, with many of his solos being sublimely structured, even though he is improvising. In line with this, characteristics of his playing style include strong storytelling devices such as:

- Vocal-like blues/gospel influenced phrases

- Call and response

- Lines that function as melodies in their own right

In addition, however, in order to pull away from the bebop tradition, you'll hear him use,

- Harmonic and rhythmic repetition

- Rhythmic variation

- More intervallic scale sequences

- Exploratory motif and thematic development

- Side-stepping and the superimposition of substitute arpeggios

The tune we'll use to explore Shorter's style in this chapter is a modal blues that includes substitute dominant chords to spice up the harmony. The addition of these changes allows us to modernise the blues and play more interesting ideas using these techniques.

Iconic Recording: Footprints

One of Shorter's most well-known compositions, *Footprints* was recorded in 1966 for *Adam's Apple*, his tenth album, which was released a year later in 1967. That same year the tune was also recorded by the Miles Davis Quintet and appeared on *Miles Smiles*.

For the *Adam's Apple* session, Shorter was accompanied by Herbie Hancock on piano, Reggie Workman on bass and Joe Chambers on drums. Also check out the up-tempo version of *Footprints* on *Footprints Live!* with the aforementioned Perez, Patitucci and Blade line-up, with Shorter playing soprano rather than tenor sax.

Footprints is a modal minor blues in the key of C Minor and has the following structure:

Cm7 (or Cm11) x four bars

Fm7 (or Fm11) x two bars

Cm7 (Cm11) x two bars

When it comes to the V chord, instead of two bars of G7alt as one might expect, we encounter a series of altered substitute chords. There is a great divergence of opinion in the jazz community as to what should be played during these bars. One suggestion is based on targeting the G7 V chord that will resolve back to the tonic, so some charts have…

| F7#11 E7#9 | D7alt G7#5 |

But listen to the original recording and you'll hear…

| F#m11b5 F13#11 | E7alt A7alt |

…which puts quite a different spin on the harmony. The examples in this chapter are based around the latter sequence, with simplified chord names on the notation/TAB.

Two further bars of Cm7 complete the tune's 12-bar structure.

NB: The lead sheet to this tune is often written in 6/4 time, but is presented here in 3/4 for ease of reading.

Wayne Shorter vocabulary for jazz guitar

Now we'll look at some Wayne Shorter-style ideas you can use to expand your minor blues vocabulary.

Our first example is played over a full chorus of the *Footprints* changes. It demonstrates how Shorter can take a simple rhythmic phrase and use it as the theme for a solo.

Melodically, the idea is transposed around and also pushed outside of the tonal centre. For example, in bar one, the motif is stated with the notes coming from the C Minor Pentatonic scale. In bar two the motif is played an octave higher, then in bar three it's transposed up a 4th.

In bar four, the phrase appears to be transposed down a b5 interval from the previous phrase. In reality, this is a simple side-stepping movement on guitar. The C Minor Pentatonic pattern has been moved up a half-step and the phrase is played in Db Minor Pentatonic.

The theme then restarts, and the first three bars are restated, but in bar eight a different transposition idea is used. This is another side-step movement, this time going in the opposite direction, a half-step down to B Minor Pentatonic. This idea is revisited towards the end of the chorus.

Example 3a

The next example demonstrates Shorter's use of rhythmic variation. While there is nothing too revolutionary about the note choices being played, the rhythmic variety keeps the listener guessing, with triplet passages, longer sustained notes, and a phrase grouped into seven that cuts against the time. It's a good reminder that we can get more mileage out of the licks we know by significantly breaking up the rhythm.

Example 3b

Next up is a simple but effective motif-led line. Throughout bars 1-8, an F note is emphasised repeatedly. It implies a Cm11 harmony and shows how effective it can be, especially in a modal context, to pick one colour tone to superimpose over the harmony and to keep returning to it. Similarly, in bars 9-12, a Gb note is referenced several times, which is the b9 of Fm7.

Example 3c

The first four bars of the next example are a great ascending lick to learn over a static minor chord. Organised into 1/8th note triplets, the rest in bar two brings an unexpected "interruption" but serves to transform the line into something much less predictable.

In bars 9-12, a superimposed arpeggio is played over the Fm7 chord. Here, we are imagining that the Fm7 is a I chord and playing off its dominant 7 V chord i.e. C7. But this dominant sound is modified slightly by playing a more open sounding C7sus4 – a typical Shorter tactic.

This type of approach is common in the modal period of jazz. As a kind of antidote to the complex changes of bebop, which relied on adding extra movements or substitutions based on functional harmony, modal players began to look at each chord as non-functioning – in other words, a potential tonal centre in its own right. This opened up the possibility of playing all kinds of scale colours over a chord, which would be considered as "breaking the rules" in functional harmony.

Example 3d

F#m7♭5   **F7♯11**   **E7**   **A7**

Cm7

The next line is an example of what was referred to earlier as an "exploratory motif". In other words, what happens if we take a phrase and explore transposing it around the fretboard? It's another rule-breaking, "Let's go on a journey with this *sound* and see where it leads" approach.

In bars 3-4 the main idea is stated. The first half of the line is C Dorian and the second half B Dorian. The phrase weaves seamlessly between the two with the aid of a couple of passing notes.

Bar five continues in B Dorian, then in bar seven we slip back into C Dorian.

A different exploration occurs in bars 9-12. In bar nine, the phrase is built from the C Natural Minor scale with a passing note. This phrase is then moved down in successive whole steps until we morph back into C Natural Minor in bar thirteen.

Example 3e

Cm7

Example 3f is another example of Shorter-style rhythmic variety, where long sustained notes are blended with straight 1/8th notes and 1/8th note triplets. There's nothing too challenging to play here, but make sure you nail the rhythmic variety and allow the lick to float over the time.

Example 3f

Next we have a typical Shorter lick over a static Cm7 chord. It opens with a bluesy, vocal-like phrase, then contrasts this with the richer harmonic line in bars 4-5 that includes a diminished triad.

Example 3g

The next line is an example of how Shorter applies simple pentatonic ideas to make a compelling, riff-like melody. It's built from C Minor Pentatonic and again is about playing with rhythmic ideas that break up the line and shift its emphasis.

Example 3h

Our penultimate example is another motif-driven line, played with punchy staccato phrases. The opening lick is C Minor Pentatonic, but the last three notes (which create a Cm11 sound) are then modulated. The Cm11 phrase is restated spelling F#m11 then Em11, and in bar five Bbm11.

Is there any harmonic reason for such movements?

For the modal jazz player, the answer can be intervallic: from the outlined Cm11, the phrase is played up a b5 (F#m11), then down a whole step (Em11), then up a b5 (Bbm11) again.

But, equally, this could be explained as experimenting by moving a simple pentatonic shape around the fretboard, close to its original location and listening to the effect this has. At the end of the day, what we play is judged by our ears more than the harmony textbook.

Example 3i

To end this chapter, here's an example of the kind of flowing, undulating line Shorter will sometimes play to counteract his sometimes sparse melodic approach. Although a line like this can be analysed and interpreted in several different ways, I based it on the C Melodic Minor scale, then added chromatic approach notes to make up a continuous line of 1/16th notes. The line ends with a surprising Ab triad that, over the underlying harmony, suggests a Cmb6 sound.

Example 3j

Chapter Four – Michael Brecker

Quick bio

Michael Leonard Brecker was born in Philadelphia on March 29, 1949 into an artistic and musical family. His father was a lawyer who played jazz piano and his mother was a portrait artist. He was exposed to jazz from an early age through his father's record collection that included the works of Dave Brubeck, Clifford Brown and many more. His father often took Michael and his trumpet playing brother Randy to see Miles Davis, Thelonious Monk, Duke Ellington and other jazz luminaries perform.

Initially studying alto and clarinet, Brecker switched to tenor saxophone in high school after being mesmerised by the genius of John Coltrane. He studied at the University of Indiana with brother Randy before moving to New York in 1969 where he landed various gigs as a sideman, before founding the jazz-rock group Dreams in 1970. Randy played trumpet in this band with the legendary Billy Cobham in the drum seat.

Dreams was short lived and during 1973-74 Brecker played in Horace Silver's quintet and in Billy Cobham's own band before teaming up with Randy to form the Brecker Brothers. They released six albums together and during that time, the band's line ups read like a who's who of the best jazz-funk-rock musicians on the planet.

Michael Brecker became one of the most in-demand session players and his music had incredible range, from mainstream jazz to pop and rock. He appeared on nearly 900 albums including works by Eric Clapton, James Taylor, Paul Simon, Joni Mitchell and Bruce Springsteen in the mainstream pop/rock genre, and Herbie Hancock, Chick Corea, McCoy Tyner, Pat Metheny, Horace Silver, Mike Stern and countless other jazz artists.

During his career he collected an amazing 15 Grammy Awards, both as a performer and composer, and received an Honorary Doctorate from Berklee College of Music in 2004.

Characteristics of Brecker's style

In this chapter we'll look at the type of ideas Brecker would play over the tune *Nothing Personal*. We'll go into some depth on his strategies as we look at each example, so here we'll focus on some broader aspects of his playing style.

Brecker said that he spent a lot of time listening to guitar players and he was intrigued by the sound of bluesy bends that hover between minor and major thirds, or between other intervals. His interest in the guitar, and the fact that he worked with iconic players such as Pat Metheny and Mike Stern, perhaps goes some way to explaining why his lines transfer so well onto the instrument.

In his playing, Brecker often took a cellular idea then really explores it. It could be a simple four-note arpeggio cell ala Coltrane, or a longer group of sale tones. Passages of Brecker's soloing can often sound like etudes as explores a cellular idea's harmonic potential.

Brecker is one of the great "long line" players. Beginning with a relatively simple idea, he will gradually develop it into intense streams of 1/8th and 1/16th notes that continue for bars without a pause. His playing is so inventive that it takes him a long time to exhaust an idea, get bored, and move on!

His modern sound comes from his ability to weave inside and outside the harmony seamlessly in a way that almost sounds like a magic trick. However, Brecker is a master of making the simple sound complex. His lines often comprise fairly simple phrases and what sets him apart is the woodshedding work he did to sequence those phrases, modifying and combining them until they no longer sounded basic. One of his main practice routines was to take a simple phrase and work it through every key in a cycle, starting low and ascending through the full range of the tenor sax, using the altissimo register to complete the cycle if need be. He had an incredible commitment to getting the most out of every phrase, and that is surely something we can learn from.

Iconic Recording: Nothing Personal

Nothing Personal was composed by pianist and composer Don Grolnick who was a member of *Steps Ahead* and *Dreams* alongside Brecker, and also played frequently with the Brecker Brothers. The reference recording for this chapter appears on the eponymously titled *Michael Brecker* album of 1987, and features Pat Metheny (guitar), Kenny Kirkland (keys), Charlie Haden (bass) and Jack DeJohnette (drums).

Also check out the equally brilliant and energetic live version of this tune on the album *The Michael Brecker Band Live*, featuring Mike Stern (guitar), Joey Calderazzo (piano), Jeff Andrews (bass) and Adam Nussbaum (drums).

In both versions, the tune is played at breakneck speed, but here we're going for a more laid back, funky groove, to allow space to analyse and digest the type of ideas Brecker would play over the chord changes.

Nothing Personal is a 24-bar minor blues in the key of G Minor with a few harmonic twists, organised as follows:

Gm7 = 8 bars

Cm7 (or C7) = 4 bars

As the harmony returns to the tonic, instead of four more bars of Gm7, there are three, and the V chord is anticipated, approached chromatically from above:

| Gm7 | % | % | F7 E7 |

The V chord is further delayed by two bars of Eb7.

| Eb7 | % | D7 | % |

The tune concludes with four more bars of Gm7.

Michael Brecker vocabulary for jazz guitar

The modal feel of this tune, and the fact that it contains a series of substitute dominant chords, lends itself to using more colourful scale choices and also superimposing scales from other tonalities to create interest and momentum.

Now that we understand the basic chord changes, I think it's helpful to provide a summary of the harmonic approaches Brecker would take to navigate them:

Strategies and scale choices

For the Gm7 sections of the tune, Brecker typically plays either G Dorian or G Melodic Minor.

For the Cm7 (often played as C7), he will continue to use G Dorian or G Melodic Minor, and the latter scale pushes the harmony towards a C Lydian type sound. Alternatively, he might also outline the C minor chord tones using chromatic approach notes from above/below, then apply side-stepping movements to move outside the harmony.

For the Eb7 chord, Brecker tends to imply the ii chord of that dominant 7 (Bbm7) and will play a scale appropriate to the minor sound, usually Bb Dorian.

For the D7 chord, he most often turns to the D Altered Scale (D Eb F F# Ab Bb C) to emphasise all the possible alterations of a dominant 7, but will sometimes just use G Dorian over this chord. (Superimposed over D7, G Dorian highlights just the #5 and #9 tension notes).

With all of the above in mind, we have to remember that Brecker would often pepper his lines with chromatic notes, and this makes it hard (and perhaps less important) to decipher exactly which scale he is using at a given moment. For instance, G Melodic Minor and G Dorian become indistinguishable when the gaps are filled with chromatic passing notes.

It's therefore more important to understand that he worked within a scale framework and used passing notes as a means of creating melodic phrases around it. Learn some of Brecker's language on guitar and you'll begin to get a feel for composing similar lines yourself.

* * *

Now onto the examples.

In Example 4a, several of the devices mentioned above are at play.

In bars 1-6, first of all notice the use of the melodic motif that gets repeated, note-for-note. It first occurs in bar one, then again in bars three and five. The motif acts as the glue that holds the solo lines together. All the notes are from G Dorian (G A Bb C D E F).

In bar seven, the sudden flurry of outside notes is the result of a side-step. We're still playing G Dorian scale shapes, but everything is moved down a half-step.

Bar eight takes a different slant and implies a D Altered Scale sound (D Eb F F# Ab Bb C). The thinking behind such a move is simply to play off the altered V chord that relates to the tonic. i.e. superimposing D7alt over Gm7.

Bars 9-10 take a different approach again over the Cm7 chord. Here, the idea is to spell out triads from the key of G Minor, using chromatic notes to approach them from a half-step below.

G Minor contains the following triads:

G minor, A diminished, Bb major, C minor, D minor, Eb major and F major.

In bar nine, G minor and F major triads are spelled out, each approached by a chromatic note.

In the second half of bar ten, this idea is used again, this time with an Eb major triad. However, it is preceded by an E major triad. This is another side-step move that anticipates the phrase by first playing it a half-step above.

That's a lot of information to take in for just 16 bars of music! I suggest slowly playing through this example several times and, if possible, committing it to memory. Then think about some of the harmonic devices discussed above and choose just *one* to work on in your next practice session.

Example 4a

The next line is an example of Brecker's etude-like development of a phrase. It's all about taking a phrasing idea and thoroughly working it, while pushing it outside and inside the main tonal centre. Let's take a look at what's happening in just the first few bars, because these ideas are extrapolated throughout the rest of the line.

This time, the harmonic line of thought comes from F Major – the parent key of G Dorian. Melodic ideas are created by using the diatonic triads of F Major to form short phrases. F Major contains the following triads:

F major, G minor, A minor, Bb major, C major, D minor and E diminished.

In bar one, the first four notes outline an Am7 and the second four an Fadd9.

In bar two, this exact phrase is shifted up a half-step to produce some tense outside tones. Each of these notes has its own effect when layered on top of the underlying Gm7 chord.

The Ab note on beat 1, for example, creates the sound of Gm7b9. The Db note that comes next is the b5. What's interesting here is that although the lick has just been transplanted, in its new position it still contains a Bb note (the b3 of Gm7) which is played twice, and so retains a connection to G minor.

In bar three, the phrase is moved up a half-step again. The effect of this movement is to make most of the notes fall back inside the G Dorian scale. Only the B note is chromatic, and its effect is to imply a G7#9 sound.

When you practice, try looping a static Gm7 chord groove, then experiment by soloing over it using this idea. Create a fairly simple phrase, then transpose it around the neck to see the effect of moving its position. A half-step movement in either direction will produce some outside tones, but moving it further may produce surprising results.

Example 4b

Here is another Brecker-style scale sequencing idea. This time the line uses an *ostinato* approach of using a whole phrase like a pedal tone. Notice that the phrase crosses the bar line, so it hits those high D and F notes at different points in successive bars, adding to its hypnotic effect.

Over bars 1-4, the phrase uses only four notes (Bb, F, C, D) and is a prime example of Brecker taking something simple and making it sound complex. The notes can be interpreted as a Bbadd9 arpeggio, based on extending chord IV from the parent key of F Major. Brecker's ability to sequence those notes and rhythmically displace them takes the idea to a new level.

The drama in this line comes when it is transposed up a half-step to be played over the Cm7 chord. First, let's remember that we've just taken a scale shape and moved it up a half-step – there's no point getting too cerebral about the results. But, the effect of this movement is a string of tension notes when superimposed over Cm7. Most notably, the Gb is the b5 and Db the b9.

Example 4c

Cm7

Gm7

Next, we have a shorter, Brecker-style four-bar phrase. This lick is based around a familiar 3rd position minor pentatonic box shape. In bar one, all the notes are from G Minor Pentatonic (G Bb C D F) and the stretch outside of that box to double up the D note is done to mimic the effect of Brecker's double-tonguing technique on saxophone.

In bar two, the first four-note phrase is used to highlight different extensions of the Gm7 chord. Superimposing an E note creates a Gm13 sound, while the C produces Gm11. The repeated E note starts a chromatic run down and a parallel 4th interval on the 2nd and 1st strings means the phrase ends on a Gb note, which implies a GmMaj7 harmony.

In bar three, the Db note is the b5 of Gm7, and the Ab in bar four is the b9.

Example 4d

Gm7

The next extended line is an example of Brecker's application of the melodic minor scale. The line opens with a repeated motif using the notes of G Melodic Minor (G A Bb C D E F#), although the characteristic F# note doesn't appear until bar four.

In bars 7-8 we see a side-step movement to play the melodic minor scale a half-step above. Think of it as G# or Ab Melodic Minor. Here, it's notated as the latter (Ab Melodic Minor has the notes Ab Bb Cb Db Eb F G). This idea continues into bar nine, but chromatic notes are also introduced, so it's no longer pure melodic minor.

In bars 10-13 the G Natural Minor scale (G A Bb C D Eb F) is used to solo over the Cm7 chord, with strategic passing notes added to approach the scale tones.

Notice the obvious side-step move in bar fourteen, after which the line uses G Dorian with some passing notes.

Bars 18-19 are an example of the superimposition strategy mentioned earlier. The Eb7 chord is treated as a V chord, and a minor scale is played appropriate to its ii chord (Bb minor). Here it's Bb Dorian (Bb C Db EB F G Ab). The Gb note that appears is just a passing note to approach the G scale note from a half-step below.

Example 4e

Example 4f is another etude-like motif development. The phrase is a bar and a half long, so there is a rest before each restatement. The notes are from G Melodic Minor. In bar four, the end of the phrase is changed and a chromatic B note introduced.

In bar eight, an angular sounding intervallic phrase is the "answer" to the motif's question, and uses the Ab Melodic Minor scale.

Example 4f

Gm7

Our next example is a line that belies Brecker's bebop heritage. Though known for his modern sounding lines, Brecker was thoroughly schooled in bebop. In bar one, the lick begins by outlining a Gm9 arpeggio, then the phrase descends through the G Dorian scale to end on a E note at the end of bar two, implying the sound of Gm6. The rest of the line is all G Dorian, but with strategic chromatic approach notes targeting scale tones.

Example 4g

Example 4h jumps straight into an atonal line with some challenging dissonance. Bars 1-3 all originate from Ab Melodic Minor – a half-step displacement – with one passing note. Bars 4-6 resolve back down to G Melodic Minor, with occasional passing notes to retain the shape of the line.

Example 4h

52

Here's another lick which, when played at a fast tempo, is pure bebop vocabulary. All of the notes here come from the G Dorian Bebop scale (G A Bb B C D E F). This is a standard bebop device where an additional passing note is added to a seven-note scale to produce an eight-note scale, making it easier to solo using 1/8th notes.

Here the passing note is inserted between the Bb and C notes of the regular G Dorian scale. If you've never spent time playing with bebop scales, it's an idea is worth exploring. The Bebop Dominant scale is the most popular and widely used, but there are major and minor variants too, as used here.

Example 4i

To end this chapter, here is some pure Brecker: a motif-based sequenced lick that includes side-stepping. Again, the idea is to form a simple phrase, then displace it to create an outside-inside line. In bars 3-4 the phrase is moved up a half-step, then resolved back down for bars 5-6.

In bars 7-8 the shape of the lick is modified slightly, but the phrasing remains exactly the same. Here, the notes come from the Ab Natural Minor scale.

Over the Cm7 chord section, the idea is to use chromatic approach notes to target C minor chord tones, and this is turned into a strong melodic descending sequence. In bar nine, the A note on beat 1 anticipates the b7 (Bb) of Cm7, which is followed by the 5th (G) and b3 (Eb).

The idea becomes more colourful in bar eleven. Here, a passing C# leads to the 9th (D), b7 (Bb) and 5th (G). Then a passing B note sets up the root (C), and extended 13th (A) and 11th (F).

This idea continues as we return to the Gm7 chord in bar thirteen.

Example 4j

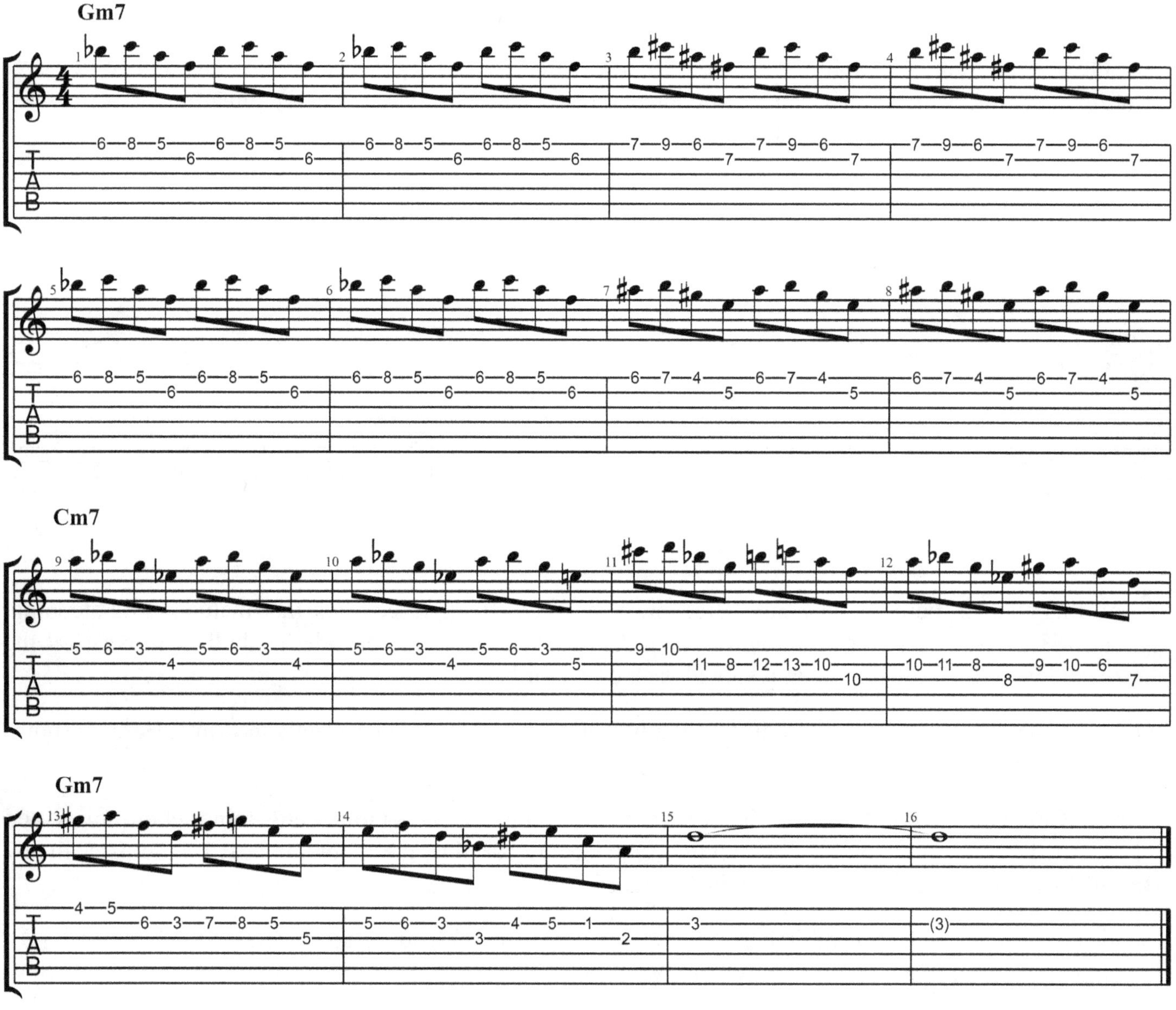

Chapter Five – Joshua Redman

Quick bio

Joshua Redman was born on February 1, 1969, in Berkeley, California, into jazz heritage. His father, tenor saxophonist Dewey Redman, played with Ornette Coleman and Keith Jarrett, and led his own free jazz groups. Joshua was exposed to a wide range of music and instruments as a child, before taking up the clarinet at the age of nine. A year later he switched to tenor saxophone, which would become his main instrument. He went on to become one of the most acclaimed jazz artists to emerge from the 1990s.

After being a member of the award-winning Berkeley High School Jazz Ensemble for four years, Redman graduated in 1986 and frequented the jam sessions of Bay Area pianist and music professor Ed Kelly. Despite his musical heritage and success as a young player, however, Redman had an academic focus and never considered becoming a professional musician. In 1991, he graduated with a degree in Social Studies from Harvard University and already had in place an offer to study law at Yale. Before continuing his studies, however, he took a year out.

This year proved to be a turning point. Some of his friends had rented a house in Brooklyn and needed one more housemate to help pay the rent. Redman moved in and was almost immediately drawn into the New York jazz scene. Thus followed regular jam sessions and gigs with players such as Pat Metheny, Brad Mehldau, Peter Bernstein, Charlie Haden, Christian McBride and more.

Five months after relocating to New York, Redman won the prestigious Thelonious Monk International Saxophone Competition in 1991. That year also saw him tour with some of the masters of jazz, including his father, Jack DeJohnette, Charlie Haden, Elvin Jones, Joe Lovano, Pat Metheny, Paul Motian and Clark Terry. Redman describes this time in his life as, "A period of tremendous growth, invaluable experience and endless inspiration."

Now committed to following music as his path in life, Redman was signed to Warner Bros. and in the Spring of 1993 released his first, self-named album which earned him a Grammy nomination. In the autumn of the same year, he released the hugely popular album *Wish*, which featured the stellar line-up of Pat Metheny on guitar, Charlie Haden on bass, and Billy Higgins on drums. The quartet then toured, with Christian McBride replacing Haden on bass duties.

A string of great albums and collaborations has followed. He formed an acclaimed quartet under his name with Aaron Goldberg on piano, Reuben Rogers on bass and Gregory Hutchinson on drums, and later The Elastic Band, an electric groove-based trio that emerged from an ongoing collaboration with drummer Brian Blade and keyboard player Sam Yahel. Many more collaborations (which read like a who's who of modern jazz), sideman recordings, and albums as leader have followed.

2020 saw Redman reunite his original quartet with Brad Mehldau (piano), Christian McBride (bass) and Brian Blade (drums) and release the album *RoundAgain* (Nonesuch).

Characteristics of Redman's style

Joshua Redman cites Joe Henderson as one of his great influences, but another saxophone legend takes the top spot as his primary inspiration – Sonny Rollins. Many have called Redman the natural successor to Rollins in terms of his improvisational style.

Redman has been called "sublimely lyrical" by jazz critics and expertly balances a love of the bebop tradition with a forward thinking, post-bop view of harmony, coupled with the desire for exploration and new creativity.

Redman is a master of motifs and their thematic development. While he may go on a soloing journey that weaves around the harmony, he somehow always manages to hang on to the melody. Sometimes, he might state just one or two ideas as the theme for his solo, then creatively explore them from all angles to tell a compelling story.

One of the outstanding aspects of his style is his phrasing and harmonic grounding, which we'll explore in the licks that follow. As a player, he is incredibly adept at spelling out the harmony, while improvising inventive lines, and many of his licks are sublimely structured – a masterclass in playing changes. All of this is tempered by a solid understanding of rhythmic variety, evidenced by his occasional playful lines.

Iconic Recording: In Walked Bud

In Walked Bud is a classic jazz standard, written by Thelonious Monk in 1947. The "Bud" in question was Monk's great friend, pianist Bud Powell, and the melody hints at the Irving Berlin tune *Blues Skies*. It has been covered many times by numerous artists.

Our reference recording for this chapter is Joshua Redman's 2016 recording from the album *Nearness,* a duet outing with pianist Brad Mehldau. Being accompanied just by piano, rather than a whole band, allows Redman the freedom to explore his motival ideas with plenty of space. Listen to the album and you'll hear the two players beautifully support and respond to each other.

Like many jazz standards, *In Walked Bud* is an AABA structured tune. Written in the key of Ab Major, it is organised as follows:

A Section

| Fm | FmMaj7 | Fm7 | Bb7 Eb7 |

| Ab6 F7 | Bbm7 Eb7 | Ab6 |

The A section has first- and second-time bar endings. The first time around, a minor ii V leads back to F minor:

| Gm7b5 C7 |

The second time bar resolves to one bar of Ab Major. This is followed by the B Section.

B Section

| Fm7 | % | Db7 | % |

| Fm7 | % | Db7 | Db7 C7b9 |

To conclude the tune, the A section is repeated. For solos, the first-time bar is used each time to roll around to the head, and the last time the Ab6 is played (or sometimes a surprise Gb6add9 chord, in true quirky Monk fashion).

Joshua Redman vocabulary for jazz guitar

These examples focus on Redman's ability to construct flowing lines that clearly outline the underlying harmony while never losing sight of the main melody.

Example 5a is a prime example. This line navigates the harmonic structure of the tune, laying down clear markers regarding what is happening in the chord changes, but hints at the original melody throughout, without ever actually playing it.

In bar one, the F minor chord is outlined and bar two uses just the 5th (C) and the all-important major 7 (E) of FmMaj7 to signify the presence of that chord.

The theme continues in bars 3-4. In bar three, Fm7 is outlined, and in bar four just two notes are used to indicate the 3rd and b7 of Bb7. For the Eb7 chord, we could play a similar thing, but after the Db (b7) note, the B, rather than Bb note, is a chromatic approach that anticipates the 3rd of the Ab6 chord.

Bars 5-7 feature a typical Redman-style swinging bluesy line. In bar eight a couple of passing notes make up a bebop line (notice the use of an E over Gm7b5 to create an extended minor 13b5 sound) with a chromatic run up to the 3rd (C) of F minor to end.

Example 5a

The next example shows how Redman might develop the simple storytelling approach of the previous line and work it into a more sophisticated melodic idea.

In bar one, the purpose of this line is to target the C note on beat 1 of bar two, the 5th of FmMaj7. We get there via a chromatic approach. Knowing that a Db note will feature in the run up to C, a lower Db is played right on beat 1 of bar one. Although that note occurs in the Ab Major scale, it shouldn't really be there, as it has nothing to do with an F minor chord, but I played it because it's characteristic of Redman's intelligent improvisational style. He often passes hints to the listener about where he's going to take an idea ahead of time.

In bar two, rather than highlighting the FmMaj7 chord with the minimum amount of information we take the opposite approach and spell it out adding colourful extended tones. The first four-note phrase combines the 5th, 13th, 7th and 9th, and the second phrase has the 7th, root, b3 and 5th.

Also of note in this line is the way the Bb7 to Eb7 change in bar four is handled. Here the harmony has been changed to Bbm7 – Eb7 and we are using the substitution idea we've seen before in this book. The focal point of the bar is the Eb7 chord and, in order to create an altered sound, a minor tonality a half-step up from its root is superimposed over the top. All the notes here are found in the E Melodic Minor scale.

In the final bar, an enclosure run targets the Eb note (the 3rd of Ab6), then the root.

Example 5b

Next up we have another sophisticated line reminiscent of how Redman (much like Michael Brecker) takes an idea and develops it into something so melodically well-formed that it sounds like a pre-rehearsed etude.

In bar one, following a lead-in chromatic approach note, the F minor chord is spelled out. In bar two, we avoid playing the F note, and the arpeggio is sequenced using the b3, 5th and 7th. In bar three, the Bb note hints that the underlying chord could be Fm11.

In bar six, the Bbm7 chord is spelled out using the root and b3 with an extended 9th. The Bb minor theme continues over the Eb7 chord this time, with the notes implying a Bbm6.

Example 5c

Something that becomes apparent after listening to a few Joshua Redman solos is how he makes use of the range of his instrument to maintain interest when playing long lines. This next line is an example of his undulating line composition, which occasionally jumps between registers, manifesting itself as string skips on guitar.

The jazz guitarist Lage Lund has said that often he thinks in terms of two voices when he plays – a higher register voice and a lower register one, each of which are playing melodic lines. He switches between voices to construct his lines and the result is a type of counterpoint effect. Redman uses a very similar approach. Check out this etude-like take over the A Section.

Example 5d

Example 5e demonstrates how Redman sounds at his most "Rollins". It's a motif development that uses lots of space, takes a strong rhythmic approach, and is more intervallic than previous examples.

Example 5e

By contrast, we return to a more complex line for the next example. In bars 1-3, the F Melodic Minor scale is used throughout. The A on beat 4 of bar two doesn't belong to that scale, it is part of an enclosure lick that is targeting the Ab note on beat 1 of bar three.

Bar four continues with F Melodic Minor scale notes over the Bb7 chord, where the C and Ab note choices suggest a Bb9 sound. From there, it's easy to side-step down a half-step to play a similar pattern over Eb7. In its new location, the two-note phrase highlights the 3rd and #5 of Eb7.

In bars 5-6 we play another side-stepping idea, in which the four-note phrase stated at the beginning of bar five shifts down a half-step in the latter half of the bar, and down a further half-step over the Bbm7 chord in bar six.

What is the effect of this shape-driven idea?

First of all, the phrase spells a Cm7 arpeggio. The idea here is to draw from the diatonic arpeggios found in the parent key and use them to play over any other chord from the parent key. The harmonised Ab Major scale contains the following 7th chord arpeggios:

Abmaj7, Bbm7, Cm7, Dbmaj7, Eb7, Fm7 and Gm7b5

It's very common for chord iii to be substituted in place of chord I. Take some time to experiment with all the other arpeggios from the parent key, because each one creates a different colour.

Moving this arpeggio shape down a half-step (now effectively a Bm7) has the effect of creating a series of colour tones over the Ab6 chord. The A, D and B notes are the b9, #11 and #9 respectively, while the F# is the tense b7, which should be a major 7.

In bar six, we move the shape down another half-step to play it over Bbm7. Miraculously, in this context all the notes are chord tones and occur b7, 5th, b3 and root. As we've seen with other players like Brecker, it's worth experimenting to move phrases around the fretboard to see what happy accidents can be created.

Example 5f

Example 5g shows how Redman's mastery of phrasing and rhythm controls the space in his lines. During the first five bars of this example space is left for the listener to digest the melodic ideas before three bars of 1/8th notes spell out a more complex idea. I've said it before, but it's worth saying again: try singing your melodic lines because you'll be forced to take a breath. Saxophonists are compelled to do this because of the physical nature of their instrument, but guitarists are often guilty of "not breathing" between phrases.

Example 5g

The next line reiterates the concept that Redman may have many ideas during the course of a solo, but he never loses sight of the one *big idea* – the original melody. This line drops the listener small hints that remind us of the tune without ever actually playing the melody.

Knowing the melody of a standard is, of course, absolutely key to incorporating this idea into your playing. The next time you sit down to learn a standard, listen to several different versions on Spotify, and especially those performed by vocalists if possible. Vocal versions tend to be the most helpful in capturing the essence of a tune, and the lyrics will help you to understand the mood of the song and what emotions the composer wanted to convey. If there are no lyrics, then listen to a few versions by different players to hear how they interpret the tune.

Example 5h

The next example is inspired by Redman's incredible facility with motif development, which is expressed in a contemporary way by playing with the harmony and seeing how far ideas can be pushed. Here, the phrasing and rhythm of the notes is maintained as the motif is explored over each individual chord.

Notice in bars 1-3 that each line begins with a chromatic approach note that targets a chord tone. In bar one the F root is the target, in bar two it's the defining major 7th E, and in bar three it's the b7 (Eb) of the Fm7. This simple idea is kept up for the entire lick!

Example 5i

To end this chapter, here is a complete solo over a full chorus of the changes to *In Walked Bud*. It brings together all the ideas we've discussed in this chapter. See if you can spot the devices being used as you play through it.

Example 5j – Full Solo

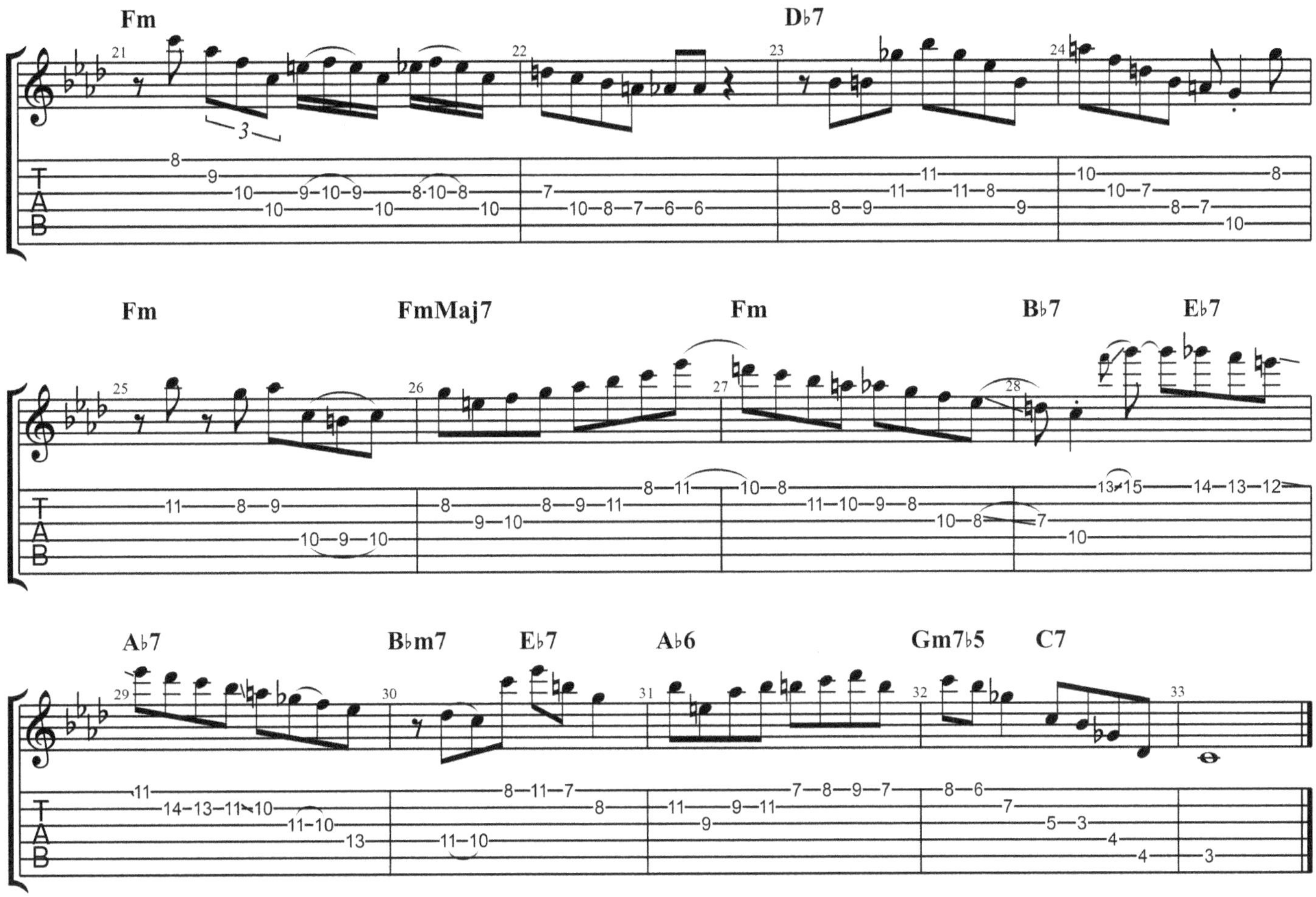
Fm
D♭7
Fm
FmMaj7
Fm
B♭7
E♭7
A♭7
B♭m7
E♭7
A♭6
Gm7♭5
C7

Chapter Six – 2 x Bonus Brecker-style Solos

To end our exploration of modern post-bop vocabulary, here are two bonus solos to learn in the style of Michael Brecker.

Played over the 24-bar minor blues changes of *Nothing Personal* these are at a faster tempo than before. Take your time with them and if you encounter any tricky passages break these down into manageable chunks and work with them slowly to establish a comfortable fingering/picking approach.

I won't break down and analyse these solos, but they encompass a range of the techniques we've discussed in detail in this book. Have fun and always be prepared to push your playing to the next level.

Example 6a - Solo 1

Example 6b - Solo 2